Amnesiac

Amnesiac: Poems

Duriel E. Harris

The Sheep Meadow Press
Riverdale-on-Hudson, New York

Designed and typeset by The Sheep Meadow Press
Distributed by The University Press of New England

Cover Art: "Datura Flower" by Dick Hoge
Author photograph by Lillian Bertram

All inquiries and permission requests should be addressed to the publisher:

The Sheep Meadow Press
PO Box 1345
Riverdale, NY 10471

Library of Congress Cataloging-in-Publication Data

Harris, Duriel E.
Amnesiac : poems / by Duriel E. Harris.
    p. cm.
ISBN 978-1-931357-74-6
I. Title.
PS3608.A7826A46 2009
811>.6--dc22
                                        2009022227

Acknowledgments

With special appreciation for the generous support of individuals and audiences who heard soundings of these poems in their many iterations. Special thanks as well to the organizers and staff of the following reading series and performance venues who facilitated such soundings: African Festival of the Arts—Chicago, Bowery Poetry Club, Chicago Cultural Center, Elastic Arts Foundation, Estrada Poznanska, The Fuzion Project, Guild Complex, Leadway Gallery, Links Hall, MiPO at Stain, Myopic Poetry Series, NCPR Open Studio, New Langton Center for the Arts, The Overture Center for the Arts, Pitt Contemporary Writers Series, Poet's House, The Poetry Center—Chicago, The Poetry Center—San Francisco, The Poetry Project, Poets Out Loud at Lincoln Center, Segue Reading Series, Studio Museum in Harlem, Walker Art Center, University of Alabama Libraries Reading Series, University of California at Santa Barbara Multicultural Center and Fred Anderson's Legendary Velvet Lounge.

Many thanks to the editors and staff of the following journals and anthologies in which versions of these poems first appeared: *ACM/Another Chicago Magazine, Encyclopedia, Fence, Mandorla: New Writing from the Americas, milk magazine, MiPOesias, Mixed Blood, nocturnes (re)view of the literary arts, PMS poemmemoirstory, The Ringing Ear: Black Poets Lean South, Shampoo, The Sour Thunder HypertexteMixes, Spoken Word Revolution Redux, Stone Canoe, WarpLand, Works and Days,* and *Xcp: Cross Cultural Poetics.*

The poem "black hand side" was published as a part of the *10x10* limited edition series commemorating the 10th Anniversary of Cave Canem.

The poem "self portrait with body" was published as a limited edition broadside commemorating a reading at The University of Alabama Hoole Library. The broadside was designed, illustrated, and printed by Ellen Knudson, Crooked Letter Press.

My abiding gratitude to those colleagues and mentors whose gifts of focused attention and collaborative energy have sustained me. I am most especially indebted to Dawn M. Joseph, tammy Ko Robinson, and Edward Wilkerson for contributions to the collection's design and further to Dee Alexander, Michael Antonucci, Mwata Bowden, Tisa Bryant, Toi Derricotte, Latasha N.

Nevada Diggs, Cornelius Eady, Douglas R. Ewart, Nick Flynn, Krista Franklin, Reginald Gibbons, James C. Hall, Monica Hand, Terrance Hayes, Tyehimba Jess, Karma Mayet Johnson, John Keene, Yusef Komunyakaa, Quraysh Ali Lansana, Dawn Lundy Martin, Dushun Mosley, Mankwe Monika Nkatuati Ndosi, Aldon Lynn Nielsen, Mendi+Keith Obadike, Jeff Parker, Hermine D. Pinson, Sterling D. Plumpp, Pedro Ponce, Sonia Sanchez, Darius Savage, Giovanni Singleton, Sidney Sondergard, and Ronaldo V. Wilson. With special thanks to Stanley Moss for his interest and support of the work.

As always, more than love to my parents and family and we who chose one another.

I gratefully acknowledge the following institutions for their support: The Cave Canem Foundation, The MacDowell Colony, The Pan African Literary Forum, St. Lawrence University, and The University of California Santa Barbara, Center for Black Studies.

Preface

Amnesiac is a furious metaphorical campaign to seize meaning from human violence and suffering. Duriel Harris works with and against language as she rushes through forms—poetic lines, prose, musical scores, charts, visual images, typography as visual medium. And she also works with and against her materials—innocence and brutality; history and literature; endured pain and celebrated resilience; allusions and aversions; African, African American, and Afro-Cuban words, codes and deeds. In this book, as in too much of life, experience and language are irreconcilable, and each is irreconcilably self-contradictory. Violent destroyers seek no understanding, and their victims can find none, but *Amnesiac* does not forget what it knows. It is a thrashing, decentered collection of changes so rapid that it is linguistically iridescent.

Reginald Gibbons

for all our kin

I am a woman committed to
a politics
of transliteration, the methodology

of a mind
stunned at the suddenly
possible shifts of meaning—for which
like amnesiacs

in a ward on fire, we must
find words
or burn.
                    —Olga Broumas, "Artemis"

The body is a source.

—Eavan Boland

Contents

Sleep

                                        Dark.

God's skirts, light's excess
magnifies and eclipses.

Sheets of past exhale
my name, low song
punctures memory into weeping.

a prayer: o
my body, and a white nest of applause
                                stings the periphery.
What roars beneath the bed also spirals between parked cars,
a chorus sputtering motors, frayed resolve.

The message is a tear in the paper,

brain and skull puréed inside a helmet,
                massacre lullaby.

                        The mechanism is the image,
                        selected, cut and framed.

I shut it out, subtract.

Unfurled
The Pain-Body Speaks in Repose

i.
Where there is will, apathy and subjection
I am a faithful servant gone to market.

ii.
Gradually, purity—the blood idea—
will soften the contour of each living man,
drawing out the will to power, to command
enormity, vagrant and enrapt, a body sorely knit
like mine, a mighty swirling column
of refuse and scraps.

To see after it and see to it, I am.
That I am I cater annihilation. I will
break your restless walking to flickers
and taps. Burrowing, I torment dreams
and waking fears, clear wind
and notches of smoke. I scrounge
and make do, scuttle and mangle
and roam to make barren. Seeking,
I find—the inflammable ligature
—the human thread
and use it as fuel.

iii.
Yet, who can but come to table at the invitation of a feast?

Charity compels labor
and conscience begs no pardon.

Traversing the earth, I whistle and build,
chisel and chirr, amassing
roving death dealers' porous ghosts
and memories of the bewildered dead's pathetic squealing.

I nurse hatreds to dress hatreds,
marshal squadrons of dogs, locusts, and carrion birds
and send them forth with poignant clarity (they shall run
and not be weary). O drunken momentum. O sun-baked splatter.

Insatiate, they, too, shall devour.

iv.
Come and celebrate with me this triumphant living sin.

In praise of its stench
low and spiraling downward,
hawkish whir, nexus of the eye
fallen to seed the ground.

In praise of its deep structure
and obscenity, its flesh wager
and decomposition wilding, wagging
into subtle architecture, fingers, isolated
joints, remnants of suppurating wounds.

In praise of its bald-faced supplicants
coaxing the unseen with jars of jaw fragments
and teeth, hair and scalp wrapped in brown
butcher paper, and trinkets, obstinate vertebrae
brushed a metallic blue, the bony burr
of hatchet holes and skulls in rows like shoes for sale.

Enduring Freedom

And what I assume you shall assume
For every atom belonging to me as good belongs to you.
—Walt Whitman, "Song of Myself"

Enduring Freedom: American Doxology

I am the hate that I oppose
That which I am not is naught

I am the chain of acts, of generations
I glorify myself and do not waver

For I am might
I shall be magnified

My enemies are as but dust
I wash from my feet

Fall on thy face
Bring of thyself to slaughter

For here am I
Stone seat of holiness

Awful in my killing clothes
Magnificent and melodious

—October 7, 2001

Defense

Mind glut
crowded with teeth and reason,
stuffed gum to tonsil with hunger.
Naked mask: we share war like a cake;
its fleshy creme solders cheeks and fingers.
Casually we tour, each sticky smear;
pity: sweet pillory, sucking overheard.

Memory is arrogant, ill-conceived.
Aspiration of a fouled sheet.
Enemy: simple word made empire.

Enduring batter. All among us
zealots of fatted tongues.

Desire, knot,
yeasty cantor, bellows grit
and plaque, herniating rapture.
All among us knead its pulsing vessel.

Academy of War

massed into a dense cluster
virtue requires an object
                    to affirm

tearing away the surface against which it is seen
to flower at the axes

its worn casements hang,
its ceilings vault
                    to instruct
by simple division
each belligerent's endeavor

....

the pledge: to shoulder
consent, so named from the shape of feeling
a statement of due interest
brindled, steadfast under duress
                                    proximity
once, but no longer the perimeter

....
                far afield,
bodies pile up, huddle unfiltered
against the grains of a noisy image

                far afield,
summer rains complicate by flood, by stink, by bloat

....

what is a wound to a dead thing?
a metal rod, a cable, a canister,
a word sculpted of leaky flesh and brine?

the reason something is an example, a fold, a predicate,
an economy of virtual knowns, interrupts

grown accustomed to: a swift vessel moored in a rivulet

what interests threatens to spill over
and smell edits the air

Amnesty

Those not finished off
have arisen and walk
with the dead twisting
their mouths and skin.

Those not finished off
have arisen and walk
with the dead grinding their sleep.

Throw open the embalming chamber.
Its inhabitants have gone out to shovel the day.

Throw open the factory, the churches, the school.
A plague has blown shadows through their songs.

What is it? What does it mean?
What quarrel? What seizure? What scourge?

The dead bring forth from night.
The dead bring forth from night.
Hacking earth with blood
and broad, flat plates.

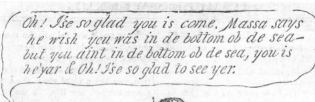

Phaneric Display No. 5: de bottom ob de sea- (June 14, 1862)

Oh   Massa

de bottom

aint   de bottom

see

Oh

you was

but you aint in

you aint in

& Oh! I'se so glad

Wishing Well

Lively march with snare drum, fife and bugle
(Traditional, Modern-era)

"Massa says he wish you was in de bottom ob de sea—
but you aint in de bottom ob de sea, you is he'yar…"
—Negro Mammy to Union Soldier
Illustration, *Harper's Weekly*, June 14, 1862

Wishing Well
Lively march with snare drum, fife, and bugle
(Traditional, Modern-era)

Chorus:
Sea bottom wid de bones de bones de bones
Sea bottom wid de bones & cutlass shine
Shanty bottom wid de bottles & de bones de bones
Shark bottom wid de nigger shank bones

Solo:
Rag spittle: Mah heart am your'n
Ah kin sang hushye babe
And Ah kin kill all yer corns
I'se a good washer wench
And cook de night thru de morn
Lawdy-lawdy Lawd Lawd Lawd

Duet (fife & drum)

Repeat Chorus:
Sea bottom wid de bones de bones de bones
Sea bottom wid de bones & cutlass shine
Shanty bottom wid de bottles & de bones de bones
Shark bottom wid de nigger shank bones

(Chorus and vocal solo in round)
(Ad-lib to fade)

from *Recollections of My Early Life*

I spent many happy hours with my black "mammy"—Sarah, our washerwoman, cook,
& maid of all work. I called her Polly—she was large & very black & good-natured,
—an ideal servant. To my delight & father's amusement I was called her "shadow"
by the darkies. Her internment was accompanied by weeping & the peculiar wails
of negroes & much sadness on my part. What bliss, after rambling all day in fields
& woods, to return to a supper of corn bread, milk &honey & after Polly had scrubbed
us well, to crawl into the lap, the high bed of her great black bosom & wade in gullies
of sleep, the patter of rain, lavender blossoms & shade. With what distinctness I recall
the great oaks, apple orchards, azaleas & grapes, the round blue hill, the great black
stove.

The bringing	
of the	total
African to America	imported
planted	into
the	North
the first seed of	America
	Estimated percent of
dis-Union.	total[1]
The bringing	
. . .	. . .

source: D.W. Griffith, *Birth of a Nation*, 1915, title card.
   Todd Savitt, *Medicine and Slavery* (Urbana, Illinois, 2002 (1978, 1981)), 32.

specimen

mulcted
a literal sea, banquet
of bodies: good ore, plenty filling
our ministrations' delicious martyrdom

to harvest curative measures
we, the great house, procure
(pox and fever catalogue)
blank black cadavers at derelict speed

[1]

Senegambia	13.3
Sierra Leone	5.5
Winward Coast	11.4
Gold Coast	15.9
Bight of Benin	4.3
Bight of Biafra	23.3
Angola	24.5
Mozambique-Madagascar	1.6
Unknown	0.2
Total	100.0

in hospital, a prayerful negro
congregation, malingering—of course
makes for robust anatomical dough
to raze a proper contagion

i.e. case [Jefferson to Waterhouse, 21 August 1801]
cultivated pustules—putrid scabs' soft seepage
—evict—puns evince—living pox
(glee:

> *The Negress Sarah, a cook, had been injected with fresh matter and took the infection*
> *mildly. A later introduction proved uneventful; our experiment, a success.*

chocolatey dessert
and brandy to aid digestion)

speleology

pulling up into   the attic crawlspace   the carapace.   The mind saw's hum-

wet metal, circling   grazing, peripatetic   upon dermis fat tissue: a solitary body's

sudden   doorframe   pose.

A body: a trick   a knot,   a dare.

§

Ssssshhhhhhhh. A woman's voice leaks, pooling in the seat of my skull just as I awaken. *Ssssuuuuhhhhhh* The woman again, scattering, her voice seed swinging out until a name's open shape casts back shadows. Zzhhgghhnn. I snore, feel myself surfacing, weedling through sleep's muddy grain.

On the pillow by my head, a thought flares, its center spitting charcoal: *there are those who want you dead; I stand among them.* As I open my eyes, the thought drags its mark across, connecting my brows. Its brittle thickening angles, absorbs and bewitches the light. In the canopy above me, I hear someone counting stones.

§

The fool washes his mouth with water then complains of thirst.

§

Discreet fragments of our time | resonate | in the eye | the mind
perception | the cognitive flicker | draws the body | in
conflicting directions: vectors | the body follows at once—exploding

There is no illusion to combat | like the real
the body | already relative by reason
of its displacement | submits to it

The line | color | shape of the world | its fragments
constituents of form | mixed and impure | a railway house
through which the body passes accumulating presence

That is what the body remembers

That which makes the body | makes the self | beyond which we are undone

§

Awakened alongside shadows, broken light papers the corridor
as memory and dream pass through one another then shrink into fasting.
Transfixed, amputated in the glare, I am a ghost in my own memory.
Ahead, at the unraveling, bone waxed baskets bark woven sacks
and the blown glass sheen of a woman's name inhales.
All I cannot unmake, crowds sweating, misshapen at my back.

§

She was speaking; someone told me so.
She was speaking; I heard it myself.
She was speaking: air forced itself through walls.

I have some living things. I have some things of indefinite shape. I have some liquid. I have some flexible things. I have some skin of an animal still on the living animal. I have some skin of an animal off the animal. I have a head still in use. I have a head off the body.

They are laid there by others.

The tarpaulin covering her body flapped at the feet and fingertips.

§

The difference between dream and reality is that of aberration and delay. The mind assimilates, accommodates, and arcs over and above: an aperture clouded with light.

In dream, the blood is never wet. It is always already a neat stain and visible, as if it cannot extend itself beyond the frame's cropped tape. The gun barrel is cold and tidy. The cigarette smokes cool to the filter. And when she talks, instead of a past there is a give, a puddle in the voice.

§

self portrait: contusion

ground down and sifted
I am bone meal drawing
a lean heart's willful splendor

bone tunnel pores reek fuel and wire
promise explodes the ventricles
drums a charge into what has doubled under

daguerreotype clips   cords
pressure pleasure pipes pints:
little dead places dance their ashes

and I char about, forgetting
until my mind flattens: hypnotized walls of light
precise registers' stroked pleats

burnt thread leavens a griefy porridge
chapped and giddy raucousness
hovers to scrub the immaculate column

I scavenge skull-winding streets
nagging toward appetite
an effulgent face oil-murked and salty

mind: mined asphalt, streaks

bliss: geophagy

Humming underwing, vast sky erupts from
dirt and gravel road. Our animal creeping returns
me, tamed, to land: every loss balanced. In the middle of
a wood, there is a water table and a well, uncovered, drinking rain.
A lull, a rumble. My throat, elongated supple sponge
absorbs defiant syllables with soft resolve;
the earth bellows, rushing in.

self portrait: fractal

Child, supper and saw: meaning gusts,
foundations wrack then settle. On the hour
gray shock thinning grime curls, tearing

muscle to increase its girth. *Take no*
pleasures. Seasoned, uneven keys slack
ragged howls through loose bone

jangle. This music, limbic thrush
drives rhythms to combust, shatters
against a bold blood barrier. Cryptic

sympathies thrash an inattentive pitch.
                    Diminished, I am all nerve.

Jump Rope

Kelly, the camel-brown girl with sprinter's calves and cornflower blue cotton dress embroidered with petals of white wildflowers, stands on one foot, then the other. She is playing a game with herself: counting double dutch rhymes, imagining the clothesline, arc then slack. 5-10-15-20. Or Chinese jump rope with Sonya and Tonya, the twins whose mother irons their ribbons. Fact: *you have to look down to be sure your feet stay clear or lose your turn.* Jump on; jump in; side to side; on; in; out. She likes the contrast of their stark white, ink black twin saddle shoes evenly spread apart. So neat, they are like Jersey heifers stationed at the four corners of an asphalt pasture. Starch white with jigsaw splotches.

In her mind, the rainbow-glitter cord stretched against Sonya-Tonya's twiggy calves is exactly parallel to the hems of their dresses. Fact: *all dresses are cut to itch the back-hinges of knees.* Their mother even insists they wear dresses to Markham Roller Rink, apple picking. And matching ribbons. But Kelly prefers the gem-like balls of the ponytail holders her mother triple twists around her just-pressed hair. They can be bartered for entrance to other worlds full of talking fish and geese. Or gazed into to tell the future. Like the crystals Aunty Myra carries in a velvet neck-purse for good luck.

One foot, the other. Now she is making a new dance. Pressing her thighs together, trying to think of anything but water. Peek through one eye, keep the other shut. Fact: *cross them and they'll stick.* She wishes the stray man would open the door—that is what her grandmother calls him. Mama has taken him in. Like the cats and their found dog, Rusty. Off the street. Off — period.

But Mama is at work and granny's house is three train stops away. So she waits for him to find something to put on. Practicing times-tables on the back porch. Her keys are on the counter by the sink, not around her neck. Seven times five is thirty-five. Double-dutch again. 40-45-50-55-60. He is sooooooo slow.   Can't hold it.

When the screen door swings open, and the scraggly man steps through the frame he sees only Kelly's nylon Crayola™ knapsack drooping by the banister.

She is squatting in the shadowed gangway when he comes looking. Counting Kelly, clutching the daisies of her panties in a bunch by her knees and spreading her feet wide: her dress, a blue and white jumble around her waist. The stream splatters down the slanted walk to become a lake in the huge crack by the street steps. She wants to gush but shame comes with gushing, so she trickles. She pats the wetness with a shaggy remnant of paper towel that had been stuffed into her pencil case. All better.

She struggles to pull up her underwear but he is so quickly behind her and without fumbling he is undone. Gripping her mouth, he snatches her in the crook of his arm. She is in the air with the gurgle of his breath. She tries to stand up, smooth the wrinkles from her dress but she can't remember the names of the flowers aren't lilies tulips chrysanthemums violets are Sonya-Tonya's favorites are like Easter no   lilies   are Easter   white and see-through like crystal and counting 5-10-15-20 is four times five pink noses of sheep or the insides of your pocketbook because babies can't fit through a boy's thing see the little hole is too little and cow's udders with tits for milking to feed their children are called calves like goats have kids and the machines yank them dry and it is over.

He sets her rigid body on the alley steps, already thinking of a hot meal. Before he zips his pants, he adds his stream to hers. He wonders why it always makes him piss and sleep afterwards.

Kelly counts to one hundred, then opens her eyes.

Thritch

i.

prickly persistent vaporous thritch
iridescent miseries crowd the throat
thistle-weed overgrowing the passage hence
and from lungs to fleshy catch pit
a brackish phlegm beds down

truth not yet said become unsaid
canopy become asphyxiant
gather blown in the trachea
to be shaped in the cut away, enisled

ii.

iodine night. girl, sixteen, dim dark hair whispering fear through a slow dream
corridor, to me, girl, fourteen, bones scraped, tendons severed and reattached, blatant
plaster feet, fresh blue white, seeping, blood turning old, turning out, sharp, shiny
serrated and thin on which a future is engraved. the hospital curtain drawn between
tight circles of pain. in the drip, muted relief, whimpering.

a girl, sixteen, a tumor like a hand about her neck
a girl, sixteen, becoming wax

iii.

It is safe here
the malignancy speaking to itself has many voices,
like a thing possessed it thirsts, and so drinks, splintering
through the larynx hording songs, imagines itself
a disciple before the altar which like itself
is an instrument—though of wire and wood

iv.

morning, a mild anesthetic. the muffled ward drafting series: hooks, poles,
boards. everything a cold alcohol swab, but dry like a surgeon's hand
not yet killing. there is no other girl to protect, no one to defend.

in her place
TO ENDURE
and a dingy ACCUSTOMED TO

anxious to walk me through it, the day thins, bearing down

Malediction

Anguish at the gate, the mind safeguarding: conjugants, convivial, taken over.[1] Emulous. Seeking. To ply. To know the wounding tool by its common names. To surge, to cry out: enormous desert thorn, apple jimson, cucumber trumpet, woody weed–oak, erect and leaf spreading flush, vigorous, lobed, toothed, broad at the mouth, this spiny fruit splitting ripe delirium flower.

Taken over[2]. To ingest. To howl lovely flower and hack.

[1] **farmer, butcher**

When asked about his participation in the events of April 15, 1994 in Nyarubuye, Eastern Rwanda, Hutu farmer Gitera Rwamuhizi is overcome by renewed compassion: *It was as if we were taken over by Satan. We were not ourselves. You couldn't be normal and you started butchering people for no reason. We had been attacked by the devil.*

[2] **schoolgirl Valentina**

Through an interpreter, schoolgirl Valentina Iribagiza relays her experience with the Interahamwe as she, her parents and 5000 other Tutsis sought sanctuary in the Catholic church in Nyarubuye: *I saw the soldiers come in, and they started shooting and shooting. All we had to defend ourselves were rocks. And our local governor, Gacumbizi, came in and stood in front of us. Gacumbizi said that everyone should know what they were there for. He said that all those who were there should be killed, that no one should survive.*

Then they started killing, hacking with their machetes. They kept doing it, and I was hiding under dead people. They didn't kill me. Because of the blood covering me, they thought they had killed me.

self portrait at the millennium

for Mamie Till Mobley (1921-2003)

(Bad medicine stalks its way to surface
catches   like dirt-latched blades:
barbed buoy,   bloated blood house
tendered skull   hole-punch to daylight;
minced cartilage toughens the brilliant chill
until hours   protrude   hard and slick.)

B a a d m e d c n e s t a a l k s i i s w a y t o s u u r f c
c t c h e s l k d i r t l t c h d b l l l a d d d e s
b a r r b d b u u y b l o o t d b l o o d h o u u u s
t e n d r d s k u l l o l p n c h t d a y l t
m i n cd c a r t l aa g e ttoouugghhensss t h b r i l l n t c h
tl h o oooou uurrrr r s p r o t r u d e h a r d n d s l i i i k

SPOILED NIGGRA IS THE MEAT
; its hearty pulp warms hands,
builds strong bones and teeth.

After

Rows upon rows and columns of people swarming between us. They come:
mass at the plough.

              And a woman
burst from the crowd flailing her arms
wailing like a convict soon to the gallows.

My child! My child! Where is she?!
Anguish, tearing and gnashing.

But no one had seen the child
for it was a city of men
              and there was a great noise

like water welled up from the ground
an issue of light

         and the body of the child
was revealed to her
open by the blade.

Theology

1.
we are brown children, 3
siblings

the only people who speak to us at school are the other brown children

none of the other kids speak to us
pink-seamed blonde and evil
eye us like something smells bad

and we are it

surrounded, we clot
the drain of the playground, we are
a wiry knot of hair

our best friends are 2 small children
a boy and a girl from the East, Muslims
always slightly dirty from work
their parents own the deli at the El train station
a wedge beside the token booth

mornings, from our kitchen window we can see them sweep
the city's leavings

one day, the police stomp up the stairs,
storm the deli, swinging
black bats and yelling
they yank and snatch
spit spin and beat
our friends' parents into clumps
of blood and sweat

so we refuse to go to school
saying if they won't be going we won't go
because we know we will never see them again
the truth sloshes over our edges
we tell it all, and it stinks like rot

then we go walking and end up
where we aren't invited, and everyone there is
moist and bubbles, testifying to the greatness
of one teacher who calls us her favorites:
her little nigglets

2.
I am late for Mathematics again. I hope no one notices.
I keep getting to school late and completely unprepared
so I don't go.

I am in 8th grade. I hope they will let me graduate.
There has been a lot of homework and classwork due
but I have done none of it: my binder is empty.

I have not gone to class more than twice all year, so I don't think
the teacher — a blue oxford shirt — even knows
I am in his first period.

3.
Last summer a boy named Germaine told me a secret.
He said:
          Anger is to feel things with fear.
In our world, we imagine
he is retarded.

4.
What do we call that which falls
                              after?
          always already?
                                        In the beginning
Enoch walked
          and was not

Who will teach me my name

"Pourmore formore PoMoFunk dunk, dun paramour" or
Duriel's Bootybone Scattergram
scatty *pas de quatre* in one act

gay-be baby, ruint lady, kiss me on my shin
nigglet gravy, savvy savory, tell me where you been

Po	Mo	Fo	Mo
sight	cite	site	s'aaight
ADD	Funk	*lu-fuki*	cartography
prefix	plus	suffix	duh fix(in)
play-me-a	holy bone	play upon	soma/germ
[phat] body	holy black	(bottle) drink	bit her batter
call&response	holy writ snatch	wholly writhen	slopely-witted:
3rd turf	Bird	re-citing	THE WORD
turbid gut	bud(dha)	incising	dull woof
coonies	darksome darky	dashing dashikis	symphonies
a. consonant	b. burl	c. gloss	d. dunnage
b. drag	c. chocolate city	d. loose galaxies	e. flashlight
c. spotlight	d. taxi	e. (sub)way station	f. crisis
d. minstrel	c. saturant	c. kitchen coil	xyz. Witness
un-making	*de profundis*	*alinear*	*de mal en pis*

crow teef, crooked speech, get down to get up   high
crow teef, crooked speech, get down to get up   high
ask yo momma an yo pappy how the spirit gets em happy
crow teef, crooked speech, get down to get up   high

[loose verbs	free your mind]	[crossroads	free your ass]
(right)	(write)	(trope)	(true)
nigger	niggra	niggah	niggaz
specter	speech	speakeasy	spectra
in the beginning was	THE WORD	and the word was	
purist stank	godownmoses	disco	neo-soul tomtom
manifest	shorthand	leaner-meaner	sweat pucker
vehemence	explicit expletive	body music magus	ellipsis
raggedy rage	they keep comin	under the seed	cipher
sulfur	sufferance	sugar bush	sugarloaf
sugarhoneyicedtea	sorghum	brake	sugar titties
danky-danky-dank	crankypedal	bio shaft	skinvention

Cousin Ara got a funky butt:
take it away!

Visitation: Pain-Body

Like vomit or vinegar
or a psychotic would-be lover's
sweat. Pressure in the armpits
bottling the chest. Circling the pelvis,
it pinches nostrils shut so the mouth must open,
crawls in and down, thickens to feel itself filling in.

Given skin it sings its name into constancy.

self portrait in desire

who thought it was a flood or an issue of faucet, or a tinny ringing
and favored the cupboards' trembling, quaking proximity of trains
and the antiseptic play: swab along rim. who, bookish, loitered and loafed,
enticed by the boy in a dream of snow, who, beastly, scurried, low
to ground, blocking the vents, stuffing blowers with down; whose mind
was a tailored maze of hare and hedgehog, rabid skunk and radiator
ruffle: a puff of heat escaping, stenciled along the surface where some refuse
and others multiply, milling.

who, begging, thought it was a flood or a surge of lava, or a chemical
bonding: a molten slur repurposed, imagined terrain spun from myrrh, a cone,
a brocade smother, twisted pine chord and altar brass. who, hard wired, fled
in human tongues, suspended, syntax and inflection, foreign intoxicant.
who, moved, heard nothing, everything from the gut splattering wet;
who, strapped in, strapped on, and became, flowed out into silicon
filling, suction.

who thought *surely it was a flood* or felt baldly arthritic, a red joint before rain
or divined reaching, nurse to the floorboards' weepy eye. who swallowed, feeling
little more than without speech, wedged into bedsag, hunting looted silver
of a future's dream. who faked, picked, and prodded into half days. who held
the heater singly to the throat to coax the slimy membrane of sickness out
into hospital for the pill, broth and gelatin, for the walking away—every letter
shifted forward seven paces—and the official papers hidden in all that crisp negro hair.

to choose the cock, to pronounce it
(to augment the mouth's labor)

to admit the queer protrusion, the lift
(your curiosity, a row of teeth—
force, there, too, just beneath the tongue)

to welcome the blood rigor, the stiffening tug
steady gaping, to bend into it
(and someone watching—always someone watches—
      who unbridles the tongue, massages the lips
         moistens the fleshy jaw)

Mine Tunnel

In the 24 hours it takes blood to set, a dream wanders the mine cavity's snug cut, caressing its miles of heavy rails, noting the grid-like efficiency of its machines: their tireless ripping, drilling, and bolting in celebration of the haul. Elongated and hollowed out, the dream represses gaggles of cough and stoic muscle, discards the idea of them like a glove dropped down a darkening shaft, converting helmets and belts, hand tools and boots, sturdy double-stitch and hardy lung to a fine black dust as light as gas.

The dream perforates and barricades as needed, blowing past sagging roofs to embed itself in the mine's solid core. Restless, it ventures out to follow the muddy sound of voices grating against its seams, clouding the precision of the longwall shear. As it slides along the coalface, it shrugs a pinch of convulsive rust into its would-be cheek and bursts into pitch, its carbon spine, dizzy and electric.

Scattered alit, stumbling deaf and unfeeling, the men the dream does not account for cluster, disfigured: rapid fire, the true skin, pocked, inflamed and pustulate, fails into sacks of kidney, liver, brain. Anoxic, breath dissociates to crags and ripples, ensnared in the dream's loose bearing. Moaning, the men flail, exhibit and effloresce, vespine crystals erupting from ditch and drain. Substance: dross heap or dredge?

Reaping overburden's steady crawl, the men effigiate themselves, burn into something resembling air.

self portrait in relief

Gilded, the jaw forgets
fracture at the pointer's tip
(red jaw, forgotten rings
inadvertent discord, picked up,
thrown into anger). To say
I feel like breaking something
and lucky find: a human face
within reach. Dallying, puffy,
deliberately adult, winter splotchy.
The pink sound of them together
fist and jaw: civil, cordial.
The face asking, *pucker?*
The hand brass, ablush.
From the flat pairing,
one accord, injury:
cozy, warm.

bad breast: self portrait as wire mother

Observe the emaciated brown body
pocked with udders and mites, the thirsty sack
dress, poorly hemmed, the mother stain
pattern, the bacterial gauge.

Postulate:
Impatient knocking, hooves trampling the solid core
door. Cameras roll down into the house. A vacuous crib
lurches into present detail.

Naked yellow-brown baby, newly sleeping
a dense rasping sleep. Behind you, a woman
in labor, midway, gathering her purse
and essentials: petrolatum lip balm, mirror,
rescue inhaler. Heading out in alarm.
More are coming.
More than one crammed into the petite frame.
More babies' pod-like fists and gummy mouths
dribbling into the bright room, arias bounding
to bright yellow windows' stucco arches.

The cluttered air plush with everyday
use and dust peaks at 104 degrees, coaching
an electrode claw, intravenous itch.

You hold the heavy wheezing head against you
and smudge its saccharine breath against your breast.
A second baby dies; a third retreats into sterility.

Portrait: Of Thee I Sing

By this pact we agree to live in the child's skin

I awaken from the dream that you are my father
To find your favorite thing holding its breath above my head.
It is an extension of you in a way I cannot be
And you want me to love it as proof.
It is curved purple with tricks:

See the way it moves by itself? you say
No hands! See what it can do?

Lazarus Minor

knees apostle : : cagey tooth
roots thickness, bald and misspelled
: splinters cud and smudge

stencil fantasy : : hidden ruler
lacquer shavings, a story she tells
: watery skin tides to the armpits

surface gloss : : sewage
easel grates, braises throat
: sweaty bursa, bends

The Ascended Black

for Bucky C.S. Thomas comma HNIC

It's hard to feel sorry for him because he's so public: garrulous preceding the even kick: slobbering the pimply ball, a handful of shiny words, his own stinking mouth. Like a tourist just in from a run, the ascended black wishes water-fallen niggers good luck. *Move along, glitterers*, he smiles, prodding. A phantom bladder represses his urge to kick again. The park bench and the postcards are real. As is the urine trickling down his leg.

His erect penis is like a camera: it touches everything and the single eye weeps excitement.

Up from. He works hard, depending on the light. His cruel little belly, all jism and orzo.

Two nations roll inside his head (one black, the other white, separate yadda yadda). It's always a shoot. The winner advances to the right.

The Ascended Black
for Condolezza Rice

And it's hard to feel sorry for *her* because *she's* so public: stoic preceding the even kick: fingering the pimply ball, selecting a handful of shiny words from *his* stinking mouth. Like an executive out for a run, this ascended black tours the wishes of water-fallen niggers with feigned disinterest. *Good luck. Now move-along, senators*! she prods, chuckling. A phantom bladder represses her urge to kick again. The lone park bench and scratch-off cards are real. As is the vitamin rich urine trickling down her leg.

The secretarial penis is like a camera: it touches everything and its single eye weeps excitement.

Up from. Unshuttered to quell the boisterous rising. She is diligent, persistent, a burning bush. She labors. Her belly rippling musculature. Her hands, a sphincter releasing tension into the air.

self portrait as negro girl

the desire to belong
extracts what no one knows
remains, leaving enough to make
eloquent my polite decay

Black Hand Side

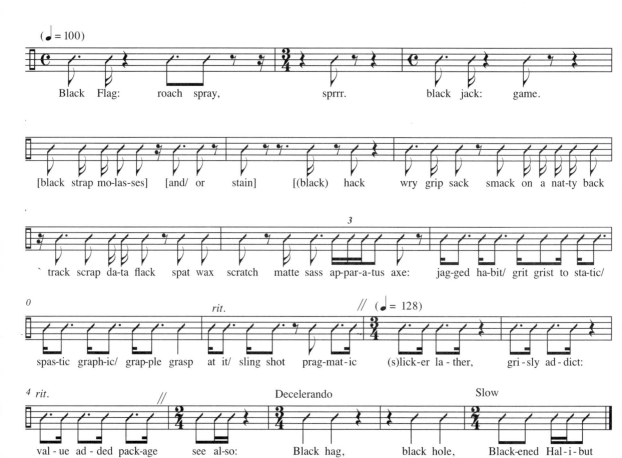

black hand side

Black Flag: roach spray. sprrr.
black jack: game.
[black strap molasses] [and/or stain]
[(black) hack—wry gripsack—smack on a natty back track—
      scrap data flak—spat wax scratch—matte sass apparatus axe:
      jagged habit/grit grist to static/ spastic graphic/ grapple
      grasp at it/ sling shot pragmatic—

      (s)licker lather, grisly addict: value added package

see also: Black hag, black hole, Blackened Halibut

—WRAITH

Guillén, Nicolás

There is no head above that of a snake;
and there is no wrath above that of an enemy.

"Sóngoro consongo, mayombe—bombe," canto para matar.

. el appellido. ether. priestly.

The head of the snake is hidden in the manifold
language of its curled length. Beneath it,
the true word, like the true skin, nests,
forced underground.

Sóngoro consongo.

        Alone in her thoughts, she scratches her scalp. Her breath stains
the vanity mirror and dandruff flakes propel themselves up in clouds,
then parachute to safety, blanketing the faucet, basin, and counter.
She shakes a battalion from her hand and considers the pieces of herself
that have dived into the crack behind the sink. And what of the bits
of fingernail, the hardening white edges of cuticle, the scabs?

A body's growth in excess, expendable.
She wonders if that is how the rest of the world sees *her*.

. beaucoup grave.

(Canto para matar.)

Certainly they *see* her or at least the form of her
                              —her height, her gait—since there's always a nod,
a smile, or a prolonged stare. An occasional stalker
                        in the mall. She wonders how they receive her name
when it moves alone, its foreignness uncomplicated
                              by the combination of her features. Dishwater hair,
yellow-brown skin, ample lips, cheekbones
                        high and flat, square jaw, dimpled chin.

Mayombe—bombe

    —mayombé.

    So is a word better than a gift
with a gracious man. Its strange
    repetition sanctifies the mouth.

    . taking on. an additional soft "g" or "j" as in giraffe.

    (Sensemayá! Sensemayá!)

    . an intimate frame.

Raiding the cabinet under the sink for Comet and a sponge, she is struck
by the unfamiliarity of the objects she finds there: a congress of plastic
bottles and aerosol cans: hair gels and holding sprays, detergents
and deodorizers, all coated with dust. On the right, a damp roll
of toilet paper. Behind it, a can of industrial strength cleanser
and a balled rag,

dried stiff, the size and color of her fist.

(.   .)

(Canto

para matar.)

.)

She thinks of the tumor newly razored from her mother's belly, its tight mass
unfurling in a jar of formaldehyde on a shelf in the hospital pathology lab.
She thinks of the yellow-pink pear-shaped body her mother will eventually donate
to science, its oily residue, its tubes, dyes, and bandages, its bloating, the bleach froth
marshalling blood to disinfection. And the odor:
    tendrils of stink climbing skyward and as far into the ground, taking hold.

                                                    . tangential and immediate.
                                                              vosotros.
                                                               an ink.
                                                             a bracket.

Mayombe—bombe—mayombé.

*The true word is hidden in the manifold
lesions of a diseased body. Its head and tail
bloom exactitude into its truncated middle.*

. one letter or two. accent. sleight.

Sóngoro consongo.
        Its skin

            black like an oven.

57

The white crystals spill into mounds around the faucet's splatter,
masking the dander. She notes the cleanser's dust patterns at impact
and appraises their abrasive caress. She considers the warning:
      HARMFUL IF SWALLOWED, social proof, a tribute to the way bleach eats.

She recalls the story of the toddler whose mother scrubbed his tar-black skin
with steel wool until he was raw as fresh hamburger.
And that poet, Eady, the changeling, his gentle darkening effacing
his father's hopes. How was it that the richness of her own darkness had faded,
as if one brown spot had been thinned
and spread across the canvas of her skin?

(Mayombe—bombe—mayombé.

            Canto   *para*   *matar.)*

She feels the gritty cleanser creep behind her knees and in the sweat between her
    breasts
until the thought of showering crowds out all others. She pulls the heavy curtain
    aside
and cranks the dial. A steady stream of water pounds the porcelain tub.

Sunlight and tungsten polish the radiator's armor to a blue glow; it hisses and she
    draws
back her hand. When she steps under the nozzle and closes the curtain, she
    surrenders
her body to the heat and her mind races into fog.

Savage bitch. Where's your head? In Africa?

Jose.

I don't pay you to think!   *(Canto para matar.)*

Ten years and still ringing. Her husband's voice towering over the vacuum, raging
at Lupe, the maid. His beautiful porcelain fingers swatting Lupe's headphones.
        (Sensemayá! Sensemayá!)

Can you even hear me
                over the rumba, bonbon of the congas
                                boring into your thick skull?

Lupe's pale bosom flushed, her narrow eyes closing.
                        Jose's frame blocking the doorway.
The headphones buzzing
                sóngoro cosongo,
                        one cup to another at her bare feet.

Of woman came the beginning of sin, and through her we all die.

(Sensemayá.)

(.　　　　.)

The water is too hot. She reaches for the dial, emerges
into the day's expectations to find herself
and her bath sheet damp on the edge of the bed.
They are both folded: the towel, a neat tripartite bundle
and her body, seated, bent at the waist, head between her knees.

Her hair has drawn itself into a wild afro, the occasional gray strand standing out,
straighter and finer than the rest.
                              And the heavy feeling she had upon waking
has dissolved into dizziness. If I am pregnant, she thinks…   to her surprise
nothing follows.

Mayombe—bombe,   she whispers,

                                counting the inch-long putty tassels
                                hanging like moths
                                from the valence above her head.

sometimes I pilgrim   down trouble

sometimes I yonder city   nobody kingdom kin

sometimes I water   heaven weary

sometimes I balm   over tossed

sometimes I valley   fear

sometimes I rough   shadow

sometimes I Jesus   sometimes I Jesus

sometimes I earth   sometimes I earth

sometimes I moan   under earth

sometimes I sparrow   woman stone

sometimes I harp   ~~pickaninny~~   harden under earth

sullen under earth   heavy water   under earth

self portrait with sorrow song

When and Where |0| Enter

When and Where |0| Enter

Refrain:
New Negro Uplift
River sun exodus
Banjo dream mountain
Wayside heritage
Niggerati party digs dust
Desolate bottom laughter
Berry drenched blacker
Death steps dark passing
Blues New Negro news
Well tower sing

(lemme hear ya!)

| ALAINLOCKE | ARNABONTEMPS | ARTHURA.SCHOMBURG |
(RICHARD)BRUCENUGENT | CHARLES S.JOHNSON | CLAUDE
MCKAY | COUNTEECULLEN | ERICWALROND | GEORGIADOU
GLASJOHNSON | GWENDOLYNBENNETT | HELENEJOHNSON
| JAMESWELDONJOHNSON | JEANTOOMER | JESSIEREDMON
FAUSET | LANGSTONHUGHES | MARCUSGARVEY | NELLALA
RSEN | RUDOLPHFISHER | WALLACETHURMAN | W.E.B.DUBOI
S | WALTERWHITE | ZORANEALEHURSTON |

ADAMCLAYTONPOWELL | ALBERTAHUNTER | ANITASCOTT
COLEMAN | MYNAMEIS MYNAMEIS MYNAMEIS BESSIESMITH | BONNIEC
LARK | CLARAANNTHOMPSON | CLARISSASCOTTDELANY | C
OMMITTEEOFFOURTEEN | CYRILLIGHTBODY | ELIZABETHL
INDSAYDAVIS | ETHELWATERS | EULALIESPENCE | GLADYSB
ENTLEY | HALLIEQUINNBROWN | HAMILTONLODGENO.710
OFTHEGRANDUNITEDORDEROFODDFELLOWS | IDACOX | JI
MMIECOX | MARAINEYMARAINEYMARAINEY'SBLACKBOTTOM | M
ARJORIEWILSON | MAZIEEARHARTCLARK | PAULROBESON
| SADIEIOLADANIEL | SUEM.WILSONBROWN |

self portrait (with vial & corn tash)

I know the rituals of snake jaw & skin.
—I am not an agent of radical acts,
fringed tongue, I am a word full of E's
—a cool porcelain belly, a spore,
a briny rusted lock, a passing scab,
an errant cell turning. I do not thirst
to destroy. I do not carry in my pockets:
roaches, forties, hardness, lawlessness, sloth,
the outer part. A symbol of grief & nettling
strops, I do not spew bright colors, do not
practice holy rolling. I am not contagious.
— In the path, I am the point nearest the sun,
a shunt in night, a gradual cumulative effect
—an involuntary stop, a deviation from
common rule, a macule, an intermittent flash,
a gleam, a deflected blow, a steeple, sleep
ripening in the break. (Certainty breeds
localized death, composts viral drills, partial dis-
closures, paralytic furnaces & vague complex mocking
sounds, fierce where the curves cross themselves.)
My transformational grammar, a shaking,
gray passage, in the sentence: the darkest
layer of bone, a huddled shrug, a current. I know
—the smarting parlor gait, the level, the lot,
the lurching shadow of the aeriform house
—where, upon shingles, rage once reached
into a boy & the boy into his mouth
& pulled from the root a permanent tooth.

& still I eye the lid behind the lid, translucent
refrain, the crevice, studying the spoiled needle
scrawl, the giddy fist's flick against water's
particle force.
                    —I am what is left
when the body has been thoroughly burned.

self portrait with body

inside grips
its motors. (guilt)
opens the door.
      (one hand spreads
      between breasts
      keeping in)
the room shocks: smells
of new coma. i swell
standing here, admiring
delicate cluster of griefmadeover
—a lug sculpted behind my sternum.
this is what they pulled
from the wreck.   jeweled and dazzling
it bullies me—uncovered toes vague greyblue
mummied from waist to skullbulb
            easy lazarus
loosely stapled to the bed linen

i admire the machines that guard
: instinctive cool mannerisms
digital and monitoring, use-dented
chrome chipping, ribbed black plastic
knobs, tubes, clamps, and humboxes
pulsing a breath-fight with death.

        (vacuum bag
          filling)

brittling exhalations (filling) punctuate
dark shapes of misplaced ordinary
as forced dumb muscle exaggerates
the chest. (head wants to fall
beside torso but tall collar keeps
afloat.)
     the body stiffens pushing against
a door.

there is no out
you always enter
s o m e o n e else

Portrait

Upon waking
an eye shuts.

Resin coats the soluble bodies of objects
and the mind applies itself, pressing

until even the light filtered air adheres
singly edging, drafting worlds.

I lie still in the balance, emptying into breath,
a slight movement in the dissolve, reaching
for the blue gaps between frames. I crave:

                         I cohere;
and objects cluster, worlds turn to color, and lock
into orbit. My skin adorns itself, humming
the warm mantra of closed systems.

The body is a habit I can break.

interval

So it has begun.
Spring loaded, mildly prosaic
Her feline abandon, a verb, arches naked

To again see itself:
a tidy collection of documents,
a room set aside for study,
the portion taken at one time to satisfy,
a body of standing water.

thin, slight, *slender*
spoken indistinctly   *moist*
typical   driven another way

It would be
Half-smiling, seeming to see something
chained, just inside   just underneath.

Notes

The Pain-Body, as conceived by Eckhart Tolle, is accumulated pain that occupies the body and mind. It is described as a ravenous parasitic entity that feeds on and seeks out pain.

As ritual utterance and rumination upon emergence into a next world, "Amnesty" is modeled after English translations of select passages of *The Egyptian Book of the Dead* also known as *The Book of Going Forth by Day*.

During the Rwandan genocide, extremist Hutus referred to Tutsi survivors as "those not finished off."

"Malediction" includes portions of transcribed statements and accounts delivered to journalists on camera in the PBS Frontline documentary *Ghosts of Rwanda*.

The refrain melody of "When and Where | 0 | Enter" is an iteration after the chorus of "Rough Side of the Mountain" as performed by the Reverend Faircloth C. Barnes (composer) and Reverend Janice Brown on the album bearing the same name. The title of the poem is a marker of its engagement with Paula J. Giddings's landmark analysis in *When and Where I Enter: The Impact of Black Women on Race and Sex in America*.

Duriel E. Harris is the author of the poetry collection *Drag*, a multivocal symphony in five movements. An acclaimed poet, performance/sound artist and scholar, her work has been featured and published internationally. Harris holds degrees from Yale University and the Graduate Creative Writing Program at NYU, and a Ph.D. from the University of Illinois. A co-founder of the Black Took Collective and member of Douglas Ewart and Inventions free jazz ensemble, she is an assistant professor of English and teaches creative writing and poetics at Illinois State University.